50 Questions
INCLUSIVE LEADERS ASK

ReBoot Accel™ is committed to empowering individuals and building inclusive workplaces.

Copyright © 2023 by ReBoot Accel

All rights reserved. No part of this publication may be reproduced, distributed, or transmitted in any form or by any means, including photocopying, recording, or other electronic or mechanical methods, without the prior written permission of the publisher, except in the case of brief quotations embodied in critical reviews and certain other noncommercial uses permitted by copyright law.

Printed in the United States of America

ISBN: 9298394389078

Visit us online at www.rebootaccel.com

Testimonials

"This book is an invaluable, one-stop guide for any leader seeking to authentically advance inclusivity at the organizational and community level. Via their 50 questions, Diane Flynn and Dr. Alex White present a highly accessible and practical resource that will surely unlock new awareness and learnings no matter where a leader—or workplace—is on the inclusivity journey. The invocation to 'call in' rather than 'call out' is one of many transformative take-aways from this important book."

Claire Lachance
President & CEO, ReSurge International

"Inclusive leaders systematically reap the benefits of a broadened talent pool, improved talent pipeline, greater collaboration, healthier employees, and enhanced ability to attract & retain the best talent. D&I is not 'box-checking,' it is the decisive competitive edge that will only be awarded to those leading organizations who choose to embrace the humanity of their employees."

Cecile Moulard
CEO, MixR

Dedication

This book is dedicated to everyone who has taken the step to be a more inclusive human being—leader, colleague, and friend. Thank you to our clients who support us and challenge us, and with whom we continue to grow. This work has no finish line.

Contents

Foreword 9

Our Journeys 13

For Leaders and Managers 19

Key Concepts 33

Skepticism 47

Being Inclusive at Work 59

Being Inclusive Outside of Work 73

Gender Identity/Sexual Orientation 85

Global Awareness 93

Inclusive Language Guide 105

Inclusive Practices 107

Foreword

Chris Riback

Diane Flynn and Dr. Alexandria White have written a most important book at a most important time.

We live, quite clearly, in a period of systemic, even revolutionary, change. We see it in obvious and subtle ways. Degrading behavior is no longer tolerated. Patronizing speech is shunned. Old hierarchies are being reordered. And like everything that occurs in this technology age, the change is happening at the fiber-optic speed of a viral video or devastating social media post.

Such evolutionary change, of course, means new, wonderful, and long overdue opportunities are being born every day. Social or workplace limitations based on race, sex, gender, birthplace—you name it—are no longer ignored, legally or morally. Each of us has the right and expectation to be judged solely by our ability and in the full context of what we bring to any position. It's an exciting, unique moment in history.

But to be fair, it's also really, really confusing.

What, exactly, can I say? What can't I say? When? Why? Whose values take precedence? Which values? How can any of us—

even at our most well-meaning best—know the "rules" when the rules seem to change with every tweet?

What we all could use right now (besides a deep breath!) is a roadmap: not a mandated list of do's and don'ts that dictates how to behave, but rather a nuanced guide that helps us understand.

And that's exactly what Diane and Alex provide.

This book raises the questions we all have, as well as the ones we didn't even know to ask. By taking the real-life inquiries they've heard in their groundbreaking work with many of this country's leading companies and foremost leaders, Diane and Alex use plain language, simple truths, and deep empathy to help business leaders and the rest of us make sense of this confusing, dynamic, extraordinary, and revolutionary period.

The cause is a just one. For any business to succeed, skillful navigation is required. More importantly, for our society to succeed—from the workplace to the playground, from the school board meeting to the shopping center—we must connect. We must meet others where they are, taking the time to understand not "what" they are, but instead "who" they are.

As a friend and colleague to Diane and Alex, we often discuss and debate the issues that animate the questions they address here—issues of intent, action, interpretation, and inclusion. We seek to explore the tensions that inevitably exist between commercial enterprise and individual expectations, from the hybrid workplace to the role of mentorship to the hiring process. I've learned a great deal from them. With this book, you can too.

In fact, I hope that readers see this book the way I see my engagements with Diane and Alex: as an on-going conversation. In the rapidly changing global work and social environment in which we live, conversation—a continuing series of questions and answers, followed by new questions and answers—must provide our way forward. For example, instead of presuming another's intentions, perhaps we could simply ask?

Indeed, among the many lessons I've taken from our conversations is this one: sometimes the path to understanding oneself comes from also understanding others.

Luckily, Diane and Alex are here to help.

Chris Riback
Co-Founder, Good Guys Media

Our Journeys

In today's ever-changing cultural environment, this book aims to educate and enlighten readers to help them become more inclusive leaders, colleagues, and friends. We know that the best work gets done when people are engaged, valued, and seen—and it takes intentionality and continued learning to ensure that this happens. Our approach in this people-centered work is to "call in" not "call out," to assume good intentions, and to meet people where they are to advance their competencies as inclusive leaders.

For additional resources, we've included links to our podcast, Call In, which focuses on supporting leaders to navigate in today's fractured and often polarized culture and to lead with empathy. As Dr. Condoleezza Rice has said, "You're never done trying to get better."

The questions in this book were all asked during ReBoot Accel's Inclusive Leadership sessions, informal conversations, and workshops facilitated within various organizations. They are raw, real, and thoughtful and each has been taken seriously. We welcome your responses and invite new perspectives to be shared, in the spirit of mutual growth and understanding.

Dr. Alexandria White and Diane Flynn are passionate about creating cultures of belonging. This book is a labor of love in their desire to create a more just and inclusive world.

DIANE'S STORY

As someone who has been a member of the "dominant group" most of my life, I understand the natural inclination to remain in one's comfort zone. It is human nature to want to preserve the positive experiences we've had, and it's often the easier path to take. I am White, cisgender, heterosexual, college educated, financially secure, and well-connected, with plentiful opportunities. However, the more I have come to recognize the extent to which many people lack these advantages, the more I realize that if I want to create positive change in the world, I must be willing to step out of my comfort zone and embrace discomfort in order to bring about growth and change for a greater good.

During my time working for the Boston Consulting Group (BCG) in the mid-80s, I frequently experienced being an "only." On one team, I was the only woman working with our client team on developing a next-gen feminine hygiene product. At the age of 21, I was the subject matter expert in the room solely because of my sex. Looking back, I see how laughable that was, but it also highlights the power of diversity in innovation. In the past two decades, the influx of female founders into that industry has led to remarkable progress in women's hygiene products.

Fortunately, I had a strong female mentor and sponsor at BCG, Indra Nooyi, the only female partner at the time and who later served as CEO of PepsiCo. She gave me indispensable advice, encouragement, and support. I learned firsthand the value of having a visible woman role model, a sponsor, and a caring mentor.

As a result of those experiences, empowering women has been a focus for me for the past decade. It was the impetus for starting ReBoot Accel, a women-owned, women-led consulting group that was initially founded to help women return to the workplace after a career pause. Then came a turning point. After watching the eight excruciating minutes capturing the inhumane murder of George Floyd in 2020, I wondered what I was doing for other underrepresented groups. And the answer…not enough.

After being connected with my now professional partner Dr. Alexandria White, I stretched into an often uncomfortable space—heightening organizational awareness of the importance of inclusivity and recognizing individual and collective blind spots. I certainly see my own on a regular basis. This work has humbled me. When I was young, I thought I knew most everything. But with each passing decade, I realize how little I really know—especially about the lived experiences of others. Along with humility, I have learned the importance of extending grace. In my opinion, these are the two things this world needs a whole lot more of right now.

I hope this book helps open your eyes to the need for a world that affirms each person's sense of belonging, as well as offering opportunities to take your own small steps to creating such a future.

ALEX'S STORY

On February 26, 2012, Trayvon Martin was fatally shot in Sanford, Florida, an event that deeply impacted me. I grew up with five brothers on the South Side of Chicago, and one of them was the same age as Trayvon. Following George Zimmerman's acquittal for Trayvon's murder, I became convinced that the country needed to engage in a sincere dialogue about race, stereotypes, and policing. I felt a responsibility to research, educate, and advocate for courageous conversations on the uncomfortable topic of race in America.

I was raised in an urban melting pot, and have always been eager to embrace people from all walks of life. I wanted to be equipped with the tools to have those conversations. As a Black, cisgender, heterosexual, postsecondary educated, and able-bodied woman, I recognize that my various identities shape how I view the world. Despite my academic and professional credentials, I have experienced microaggressions and overt racism.

I have worked in both corporate America and academia, where race, equity, and inclusion are critical to accessing opportunities and advancement. In one of my professional evaluations, my appearance, in particular my hair, was used as a reference for unprofessionalism. Unfortunately, my experience is not uncommon for women of color, and it has shaped how I hold conversations with clients about being aware of biases in the workplace.

My personal and professional experiences have led me to identify as an inclusive disruptor. To me, this means empowering ourselves to hold space for courageous and uncomfortable conversations where all opinions can be voiced, even those with which we may disagree. I firmly believe that we are more alike than different, and I hope that my life's work can inspire others to value, listen, and learn from each other. This book is a "passion project," and I hope it will help us all to come together, while understanding our differences and embracing our shared humanity.

For Leaders and Managers

Effective leaders know that creating a culture of belonging drives engagement, retention, and bottom-line performance. People pay attention to what leaders say and do. This modeling can have a positive ripple effect throughout an organization.

1. Why is it important for my company to have a diverse workforce?

Many studies have shown that well-managed diversity can drive business success:

- Diversity in a management team drives 19% higher innovation revenues (Boston Consulting Group)
- Gender diversity in leadership makes a company 25% more likely to outperform on profitability (McKinsey)
- Strong ethnic diversity in leadership produces 36% higher financial performance (McKinsey)

In addition, teams that are diverse and inclusive have 1.2–1.6x higher retention, collaboration, and commitment to the organization (Corporate Executive Board). This makes sense. When people feel psychologically safe at work, they are more likely to openly express opinions, explore ideas, and examine failures—which in turn leads to innovation, expanded markets, and better product market fit.

We have seen the performance benefits of building a diverse team at ReBoot Accel. Alex, a Black woman, brings perspectives and a lived experience that has allowed us to expand our work, the focus of which is creating inclusive cultures. Her experience in academia has also allowed us to expand beyond the corporate marketplace, and we are now serving universities as well.

In addition, her perspective has led to the development of "The Black Experience," a program we've developed to help organizations attract, retain, and advance Black employees.

Further, the diversity in the population continues to grow. A Brookings study estimates that by 2045, members of racial minorities will outnumber those identifying as White. This is already true for those under age 18. And the percentage of people identifying as LGBTQ+ is growing each year. These are people that represent your company's customers and available workforce. Any leader unprepared to lead a diverse workforce is going to be at a competitive disadvantage.

2. **Is it important to set and communicate diversity, equity, and inclusion (DEI) goals?**

This is a controversial topic, as most leaders oppose the idea of quotas. This infringes on the territory of "affirmative action," a policy that has generated criticism, debate, and litigation. Nevertheless, the companies making the most progress on diversifying their workforce are very intentional about this effort. They often announce their intent (either privately or publicly) and create dashboards showing representation by gender, race, and other characteristics, sliced by geographic location.

Most leaders seek to create a workforce that represents the communities in which they live and serve. One client who has an interest in hiring more Latin employees to serve its high proportion of Spanish-speaking customers recognizes that some markets have a very low representation of Latin candidates, and it would be unrealistic to set the same goal in those markets as for others.

When we ask companies who've moved the needle on diversity, leaders typically say it all starts with intentionality. You have to **want** diverse voices around the table. Look

Here's a sample dashboard one company uses to track diversity metrics:

DASHBOARD (SAMPLE)

Measurement	WOMEN		PEOPLE OF COLOR		BLACK		BLACK
	Current Performance	Target	Current Performance	Target	Current Performance	Target	Current Performance
Seats on Board	1 of 9	2 of 9	2 of 9	2 of 9	1 of 9	1 of 9	
C-Suite (# Reporting to CEO)	1 of 10	3 of 10	0 of 10	2 of 10	1 of 10	1 of 10	
Directors/VP/Mgrs/Branch Mgr	32%	40%	16%	20%	8%	12%	
All Employees	54%	50%	24%	35%	6%	12%	
Turnover (annually)	32%	20%	20%	18%	21%	20%	18%
Engagement Survey Score	62%	72%	60%	70%	63%	70%	68%

Key

Far from target
Room for improvement
Satisfactory

around the room and ask yourself whose voices are missing. There are countless cases of products that were developed by homogeneous teams that seriously missed the mark: pulse oximeters and automatic hand-towel dispensers that didn't recognize dark skin, electronics that didn't work well for people who are left-handed, airbags that weren't tested on women and children, and artificial intelligence applications that identified certain ethnicities as animals.

As far as communicating these goals, some companies like PwC issue public reports on how they're doing on a wide variety of diversity metrics. Others choose to share these numbers internally, but not publicly. Whichever way you choose to share them, it's important that your hiring managers understand the importance of this effort, and that employees and recruits see that you model and message your commitment to diversity.

We encourage organizations to move beyond the words "cultural fit" to seeking a "cultural **add**." The word **fit** can imply affinity bias—a desire to hire people "like" us. A "fit" may be someone whom I want to grab a beer with or sit beside on a plane, or who attended my college. Conversely, an "add" suggests someone who's going to bring a unique perspective to the table. Note that it's critical that this person subscribes to ("fits with") your organization's values: a value fit rather than a cultural conformity.

One final thought—if you want more Black/Hispanic/Other people in your organization, then don't say we need People of Color (POC). Be specific about your needs, and you will be more successful in meeting your objectives.

3. I want diversity, but I don't want to lower the bar. Is that okay?

This is something we hear far too often. When it's voiced, the first thing we ask is "What makes you think you have to lower the bar?" We never advocate lowering the standards for the position of hire, as it benefits neither the company nor the individual hired. Rather, we suggest examining every aspect of your hiring process to ensure that diverse candidates have an equal shot at being hired.

Remember that there are several benefits to having a diverse workforce. Their voice at the table can add a unique perspective that drives products, markets, and new opportunities. And having them as visible role models can help pave the way for others to join the organization.

Research proves that having diverse candidate pools and diverse hiring teams consistently results in greater diversity of those hired. One client tripled the number of women engineers hired simply by adding women to the interview team.

We've created the following 10 steps for reducing bias in hiring, and companies that follow these steps have all successfully diversified their workplaces.

10 STEPS FOR REDUCING BIAS IN HIRING

PREPARING FOR THE HIRING PROCESS

1. Create a job description and review it for biased language (the internet provides plenty of examples)
2. Identify and select a diverse interview team
3. Ensure that the slate of candidates is diverse
4. Create a scorecard so everyone interviews for the same criteria
5. Create structured interview questions that reflect the criteria on the scorecard

ADOPTING INCLUSIVE SCREENING AND INTERVIEW PRACTICES

6. Have inclusive application review and screening policies
7. Consider inclusive practices when interviewing candidates
8. Be mindful of your own biases

DEBRIEFING AND HIRING THE BEST CANDIDATE

9. Debrief with the scorecard to ensure all criteria are addressed objectively
10. Recognize and honor your role as a brand ambassador during the process

4. **How do we recruit against a candidate's self-assessment that they aren't good enough? What can we do in our job posting to get more candidates in the door or interested in our company?** Studies suggest that women will not apply for a job when they don't meet *all* of the job requirements, whereas men will apply if they meet only one or two.

   Refer to the 10 steps for addressing bias in the hiring process, shown at the end of the previous question. To expand the candidate pool, especially to include women who may not apply if the job requirements appear too onerous, we suggest carefully examining the criteria to ensure that all criteria are critical to the role. Many employers include every possible skillset or experience that would be nice to have, and this can inadvertently turn off key candidate pools.

   Also check for language in the job description that can skew male or female. Words like "ninja," "rockstar," "competitive," and "fierce" can turn off women as they don't see themselves fitting this role. There is software available that can scan job descriptions for gendered language.

5. **Is it offensive to a person of color if I ask them to join our organization? They may think I'm only asking them because of their skin color.**

   This is a common question we are asked. It's important to consider the following when having this conversation:
   - Express to the candidate your interest in expanding the perspectives shared within the organization. Share that you recognize you have blind spots, and that greater

diversity of thought and experiences will help your organization make better decisions.

- Amplify their unique skills and experiences that will contribute to this objective.
- Recognize their concern that they may be an "only," and offer ways to ease their onboarding and enhance their feelings of inclusion and belonging. Ask what they may need—perhaps a mentor or buddy would be beneficial. And don't assume who their mentor/buddy should be. Ask the candidate what would be important to them in a mentor, and then suggest some possible options. It's easy to assume that a woman would prefer a woman, or a Black individual would prefer someone who's Black, but this is not always the case. Be careful about assuming. It's always best to ask.
- If they worry about being a "token" hire, help them reframe themselves as a "trailblazer." Their presence will help open the door to more people who share their demographics and views and will benefit the organization in myriad ways. Both of us have been the "firsts" in organizations and on boards, and we are honored to serve in this capacity and pave the way for others.
- If they accept, be prepared for possible changes in culture and dialogue. Increasing diversity around the table can heighten sensitivity to gender and behavioral pattens such as racial jokes, slurs, comments, and actions.

6. **How do I help create an environment for honest conversations, with opportunities for learning (which includes disagreement) and not an environment of judgment, shaming, and resentment?**

To have these open, honest conversations, it's imperative that people feel safe. Creating trust within an organization starts with your own demonstration of humility. Admitting what you know and don't know, along with mistakes you've made along the way, helps everyone see that we are all imperfect works in progress. By soliciting and honoring differing opinions and perspectives, you are creating a space where people feel seen.

Be mindful that all voices around the table (or virtual screen) are being heard, and continue to explore your own unconscious biases. Pat Gelsinger, CEO of Intel, requested a gay man to be his mentor because he wanted to be sure he fully understood his own blind spots and that he was doing everything possible to ensure that the LGBTQ+ community at Intel feels included.

7. **How much time do you spend "pitching" the business case for diversity? Has understanding that it's good for results become less of a barrier to growth?**

   Even though there are plenty of social justice and equity reasons for diversity in the workplace, we choose to lead with the business case. We've learned through experience that people's knowledge and willingness to embrace inclusive practices exist on a continuum, but virtually all business leaders want strong bottom-line performance. The research from McKinsey, BCG, and others is clear about the competitive advantages of diversity in terms of innovation, decision-making, employee engagement, retention, and bottom-line results.

   The business case provides a strong argument that can appeal to those more skeptical about why this should be on the agenda. We see more and more companies prioritizing DEI (Diversity, Equity, and Inclusion), largely because of the research but also because a focus on ESG (Environment, Social, and Governance) is being demanded by vendors, investors, and the business ecosystem.

8. **I don't understand this concept of psychological safety in the workplace. How do I know if it exists in my organization?**

   One of the best "tests" for determining the health of one's organization comes from a 2023 article in *Harvard Business Review*.[1] The following statements serve as some measure of the degree of psychological safety present:

   - If you make a mistake on this team, it is not held against you.
   - Members of this team are able to bring up problems and tough issues.
   - People on this team accept others for being different.
   - It is safe to take a risk on this team.
   - It isn't difficult to ask other members of this team for help.
   - No one on this team would deliberately act in a way that undermines my efforts.
   - Working with members of this team, my unique skills and talents are valued and utilized.

---

[1] Gallo, Amy. "What Is Psychological Safety?" *Harvard Business Review*, February 15, 2023. https://hbr.org/2023/02/what-is-psychological-safety.

In summary, inclusive leaders:

- Don't rest on the status quo; they challenge norms and ask "why"
- Are aware of who's included or excluded (in meetings, at social events, even remotely)
- Step into courageous conversations with openness, curiosity, and a willingness to learn
- Recognize they will make mistakes, and are willing to make amends and learn
- Approach this work with humility, alert for their blind spots
- Use their advantages to help others (they expand networks, create opportunities, help others upskill, amplify voices)
- Proactively and openly seek and embrace feedback
- Continue to learn (through relationships, conversations, articles, podcasts, etc.)
- Model and message their commitment to building an inclusive culture

Check out our micro-podcasts on this topic

Is There a Jon Gruden Hiding in Your Organization?	Leading Through Adversity
Does McDonald's CEO Deserve a Break Today?	How to Drive Diversity in the Boardroom
Do Today's Leaders Have the Right Skills to Lead Today?	How to Be an Inclusive Leader: Jennifer Brown
Empathetic Leadership in Action: Julian Francis, President/CEO	How Companies Can Perform Layoffs with Empathy: Chip Conley
How to Reduce Hiring Bias	The Art of Effective Listening: Andre Joyner, JC Penney

Key Concepts

It's important to have a solid understanding of key words and phrases foundational to this topic.

9. **What is the difference between diversity, inclusion, and belonging?**

   Here is a group dinner analogy to explain the difference: **Diversity** is experienced when a group of people of varying backgrounds, identities, and characteristics who are invited to have dinner together. **Inclusion** is the welcome extended to each dinner guest, as well as equal access to what's on the menu (food and conversation). **Belonging** is the experience of being welcomed, included, and appreciated for what one brings to the table in who they are, as well as being able to make requests for one's well-being (e.g., dietary or other accommodation). It's important to note that a space can be diverse but not inclusive, and a person can be included but not feel like they belong.

10. **When we speak of diversity, are we talking mainly about gender and race?**

    There are many forms of diversity, and all are important. Here's how we think about diversity: Some aspects of diversity can readily be seen:

Other aspects of diversity are not visible, though are equally as important as those that are.

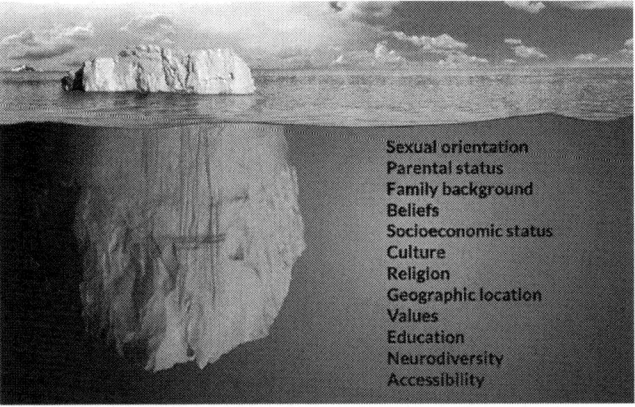

When thinking about what forms of diversity are important to be represented in your organization, ask yourself what key voices are missing. Most organizations want their employee base to reflect the communities in which they work and serve. If you serve parents and families or sell products primarily to women (women control nearly 75% of consumer spending), do you have parents and women on your team? Age-based diversity is a form of diversity that many ignore, along with its value. Currently, up to five generations work side-by-side in the workplace, and these multigenerational teams can deliver powerful products and services as a result of the varying perspectives they bring. Often, lesser attended to aspects of diversity become visible only after disappointing outcomes, as seen with some electronics companies that had early product misses because they had no left-handed representation on the team!

11. Should I refer to someone as Black or African American? And do I say Hispanic, Latin, Latino, Latina, or even Latinx?

In the United States, the terms Black, African American, and person of color are words used to describe race and ethnicity. "Black" is a term of race that can refer to people of African, Caribbean, and other Black heritages, while "African American" specifically refers to the ethnicity of American Black people of African descent. Accepted terminology may differ in other parts of the world.

"Hispanic" refers to people with ancestry from Spanish-speaking regions, while "Latino" describes those of Latin American ancestry (Mexico, most of Central and South America, and the Caribbean islands of Cuba, the Dominican Republic, and Puerto Rico). People from Brazil, where Portuguese is the country's official language, are Latin but not Hispanic, and people from Spain are typically referred to as Spanish.

"Latinx" is the gender-neutral or non-binary term for Latino/Latina (typically male and female descriptions) and pushes back on gendered language to be more inclusive. Note that Latinx is a debated term and is not widely used in the Latin community.

When making reference to someone's race or ethnicity, do so in conformity with their self-identification. When in doubt, ask.

12. What is the difference between POC and BIPOC?

POC means Person/People of Color (not to be confused with Proof of Concept) and BIPOC means Black, Indigenous People of Color. Some people object to using POC to describe Black or African American individuals because it describes a broader category. If you mean Black, use Black in your communication.

13. Who are Indigenous peoples? What is Indigenous Peoples' Day and can I celebrate it?

Indigenous peoples are the descendants of the peoples who first inhabited the Americas, the Pacific, parts of Asia and Africa, Australia, and New Zealand prior to European colonization. It is important to be aware that Indigenous peoples lived and thrived with their own distinct languages, values, cultures, knowledge systems, and practices prior to colonization. Today, Indigenous peoples make up about 5% of the world's population across more than 70 countries worldwide. Indigenous Peoples' Day is intended to be celebrated by all people in honor of the history and cultures of Indigenous peoples. In 2021, President Joe Biden signed a presidential proclamation of Indigenous Peoples' Day, observed annually on the second Monday of October. While not yet a federal holiday, it is celebrated in many cities, states, and various organizations throughout the country.

14. Are Jewish people a marginalized group? I perceive them as having money and power.

According to a 2021 Pew research article, the majority of Jewish people identify as White.[2] However, antisemitism (hostility or prejudice against Jews) has a millennia-long history, often based on an association with cultural or religious traditions, clothing, and physical features. Much of that antisemitism is driven by unfounded beliefs and conspiracy theories promoting false narratives that they control society through wealth and power. In recent years, racist attacks and violence against Jewish communities in the U.S. and beyond have been on the rise, with recorded incidents reaching a new high in 2022.[3] With those increasing antisemitic incidents comes a rising sense of insecurity among Jews,[4] as reported by the American Jewish Committee's 2022 report.

---

[2] "Jewish Americans in 2020: Section 9. Race, Ethnicity, Heritage and Immigration among U.S. Jews." Pew Research Center, May 11, 2021. https://www.pewresearch.org/religion/2021/05/11/race-ethnicity-heritage-and-immigration-among-u-s-jews/.

[3] "Audit of Antisemitic Incidents 2022 | ADL." ADL, March 2023. https://www.adl.org/resources/report/audit-antisemitic-incidents-2022.

[4] AJC Global Voice. "5 Key Takeaways from AJC's State of Antisemitism in America Report 2022," February 10, 2023. https://www.ajc.org/news/5-key-takeaways-from-ajcs-state-of-antisemitism-in-america-report-2022.

15. What does it mean to be "woke"? This word seems to be used in a variety of ways.

While this may appear to be a straightforward question, the answers that one receives are varied and often polarizing and divisive, depending on who is answering. It's an important question that deserves a contextual response.

To understand where we are and where we're going, it's important to know where we came from, and that applies to language as well. The word "woke" or to "stay woke" originated from African-American Vernacular English (AAVE) in the 1940s. Its original meaning indicated being woken up to issues of racial prejudice and discrimination. In 1962, William Melvin Kelley, a Black novelist, defined woke in a *New York Times* article about Black slang as, "well informed, up-to-date."[5] With the passage of time, the term evolved to include alert awareness of racial, social, and political issues affecting African Americans through prejudice and discrimination.

It was in 2014, following the killing of Michael Brown by police in Ferguson, Missouri, that "woke" became the watchword of Black Lives Matter in organizing collective opposition to racism and police brutality. Since that time, the word "woke" and what it stands for have evolved as various groups adopt their own meaning.

---

[5] Kelley, William Melvin. "If You're Woke You Dig It." *The New York Times*, May 20, 1962. https://www.nytimes.com/1962/05/20/archives/if-youre-woke-you-dig-it-no-mickey-mouse-can-be-expected-to-follow.html.

While some view "woke" as a progressive drive toward equity, others use it as a derogatory term for hypersensitive identity politics, like the terms "social justice warriors," "snowflake," "race card," "virtue signaling" or the earlier "political correctness," and apply the term to other aspects of progressive culture such as gender identity, gay rights, and diversity, equity, and inclusion (DEI) programs. The term "woke" has been co-opted in the culture wars, and its meaning is less clear than ever, as it is now used to forward agendas and undermine those of the African American communities the term originated in.

SOME KEY FOUNDATIONAL TERMS

Microaggressions

Microaggressions are subtle or indirect forms of discrimination, prejudice, or bias that can occur in everyday interactions. These actions or comments may be unintentional, but they can still have a harmful impact on individuals or groups who experience them repeatedly over time.

The following are examples of microaggressions:

- Interrupting or speaking over a woman or any underrepresented group
- Telling a man "You don't look like a nurse."
- Asking an older person, "When are you going to retire?"

Macroaggressions

Macroaggressions can take many forms, including acts of violence, hate speech, discriminatory policies, and systemic oppression by institutions of power and influence that adversely impact whole groups or classes of people. This could refer to overt and direct forms of discrimination or prejudice, or to policies that result in large-scale harm to marginalized groups.

The following are examples of macroaggressions:

- Believing people with mental disabilities are not capable of working.
- Redlining, which was a government-sanctioned form of housing discrimination where banks and mortgage companies refused to provide loans to people in areas identified as "financially risky." Such practices negatively

impacted Black and Brown communities by limiting their opportunities for home ownership and locking them out of certain areas.

- Jim Crow laws implemented from the late 1800s to the mid-1960s by state and local governments in the United States to enforce racial segregation and discrimination against African Americans.

Racism

The belief that a particular race is superior or inferior to another. Systemic or institutional racism refers to a pattern of social and political systems discriminating against a group of people based on race.

Anti-racism

The active process of identifying and eliminating racism by changing systems, organizational structures, policies, practices, and attitudes so that power is redistributed and shared equitably.

Bias

A disproportionate weight in favor of or against a person, idea or thing, usually in a way that is closed-minded, prejudicial, or unfair. Bias can be conscious (you're aware of it or intend it) or unconscious (you're not aware of it or did not intend it).

Prejudice

A typically negative preconceived judgment, belief, or attitude, often unconscious, toward a person or group, most often based on unsupported generalizations or stereotypes.

Privilege

Unearned social power granted by formal and informal institutions to all members of a dominant group by way of special rights, advantages, or immunity that other groups do not enjoy. Most often invisible to those who have it, privilege puts them at an advantage over those who do not.

If you struggle with the concept of privilege, perhaps this Tweet from Marie Beecham provides a useful construct:

Accessibility

Giving equitable access to everyone along the continuum of human ability and experience.

Equality

The effort to treat everyone equally and to ensure that everyone has equal access to the same opportunities, based on the assumption that everyone benefits from the same support.

Equity

Fair treatment, access, opportunity, and advancement for all people, while at the same time striving to identify and eliminate barriers that have prevented the full participation of some groups. Everyone gets the support they need.

Justice

Systemic barriers have been removed.

Equality

Equity

Justice

KEY CONCEPTS

Check out our micro-podcasts on this topic

Bias in the New Hybrid Workplace

Should Employers Remember If the Internet Never Forgets?

How to be an Ally When Women's Credentials are Minimized

Skepticism

In today's polarized world, opinions regarding diversity, equity, and inclusion vary widely. Here are some of the questions we are frequently asked about why these topics matter.

16. Why should I care about diversity, equity, and inclusion? I just want to do my work. Can't we all just get along?

If you want to catalyze innovation, retain talent, and achieve better bottom-line performance, it's critical that people in your organization feel safe sharing varying perspectives and that they are engaged in their work. According to a recent McKinsey study, over 50% of people leave jobs because they don't feel valued, appreciated, and seen.[6] Those varying perspectives that are so valuable arise from the diversity in your workforce. The safety employees need in order to share those perspectives is based on equitable treatment and a feeling of inclusion.

Creating a space where people feel they belong starts with an inclusive leadership mindset. If you recognize the dignity, value, and worth of each individual, then it's only natural to find ways to increase their engagement. You must **want** to create a space where people desire to show up, share their perspectives and ideas, and do their best work. If they hold back, you will miss out on creative solutions, fresh products, expanded services, and new markets.

Why pay someone 100% of their salary, and only get 60% because they are "quietly quitting?" Knowing how to make people feel included and heard is key to strong leadership, and it is a competitive advantage.

"Why can't we all just get along?" We can, if we're willing to take an interest in others, to listen, and to respect their unique lived experience. This does not mean we all have to agree. But we do need to try to understand each other.

---

[6] McKinsey & Company. "Why Employees Are Quitting and What to Do about It," January 16, 2022. https://www.mckinsey.com/featured-insights/themes/why-employees-are-quitting-and-what-to-do-about-it.

17. I don't get why people are so sensitive. Why does saying one little thing suddenly become a big deal?

In some cases, things do seem blown out of proportion. People are not homogeneous; they respond differently to stimuli and have their own triggers and emotional responses. It's important to recognize that your words are not always going to land the same way with each recipient.

We like to use the analogy of tripping someone. If you inadvertently trip someone because your foot is extended into their walking space, what do you do? You apologize! You didn't **intend** to trip them, but you did. We view this work similarly. When we say something that doesn't land well with someone else, it's important to focus on impact over intent. While you didn't intend to hurt them, you did. Apologize and use the experience to be more aware next time. If you disagree about the impact of your comment or action, have a conversation to better understand their perspective. Practice humility and grace, and come with a mindset of curiosity and a willingness to learn. You may not agree with their perspective, but at least you can now understand why it impacted them the way it did.

Some offenses (often called microaggressions, described in the Key Concepts chapter) are minor and unintentional. Others are egregious and unacceptable. The categorization of comments on this spectrum can vary depending on the listener, as everyone brings their own emotional disposition and unique lived experiences to the conversation. For instance, a person may not mind being asked about their accent the first time, but being asked repeatedly, despite being a native resident, can make them feel like an outsider who does not belong.

18. Might a consuming interest in diversity and inclusion in the workplace slow us down and make us less productive?

Hiring diverse talent and being inclusive does take more time. Ensuring you have a strong, diverse slate of candidates and a similarly diverse hiring panel can slow the process down. Taking the time to **listen** to these diverse perspectives can also be time-consuming. But research from Boston Consulting Group (BCG), McKinsey, and Harvard Business Review has proven over and over that having more diverse voices around the room drives better decision-making. Smart CEOs don't make key decisions when they're sitting in an echo chamber with many nodding heads. They tell their team to come back when they've had a chance to consider other perspectives. These CEOs know that this is the environment in which the best decisions are made. They recognize the uniqueness of each individual voice, and that broader perspectives lead to better outcomes.

People from different ethnic and cultural backgrounds can offer perspectives on how to take their cultures into account in products and services. Older employees may have different and more varied experiences that can inform decision-making. Those with disabilities may help you break down barriers to large groups of people. And people that are neurodiverse may approach problems in different ways.

Because language and norms keep changing, it takes time to stay current. But it's imperative to find time to keep educating yourself and stepping into courageous conversations. Some words that were acceptable last year are no longer so. And others that were not acceptable are now mainstream. For example, the word "queer" has evolved over time. It was formerly deemed a derogatory term, but has now been embraced in mainstream vernacular. There are universities and colleges that have an Office of Queer Studies.

Our suggestion is to keep reading articles, listening to podcasts, and engaging with people who have perspectives different than your own. Scan this QR code to access a list of resources we suggest to stay current:

19. I'm hesitant to give honest constructive feedback to my direct reports who are from an underrepresented group for fear of being accused of being racist/homophobic/antisemitic/misogynistic. What advice can you give me?

Any good leader knows that honest, helpful feedback is the best way to help employees grow and develop. Our best advice when giving feedback to **anyone**, independent of their level of representation, is to stick to the facts. What behaviors did you observe, and what was the impact of those behaviors? Have clear, measurable goals, and review their performance against these goals.

Trouble comes when we bring personal opinions and judgments into the conversation—"I just didn't like the way you answered that" or "I don't think you have executive presence." This is when it's important to check our biases. Did they do something to merit this feedback? Or is it based on a bias I have toward them? Finally, avoid large public venues (like social media) when sharing feedback and observations, as this is how most people get canceled. Feedback is best delivered in private settings with only those involved present.

Courageous conversations come with some degree of risk. Do it with authenticity, acknowledge that you're not going to always get it right, and vow to learn and improve a bit each day.

20. I'm not a leader. How does diversity, equity, and inclusion apply to me?

We are all leaders in our own ways. We are each responsible for creating the culture we want to see. How you treat others, consistently, makes all the difference, as you are modeling behavior for others. Think about who you mentor, sit with at lunch, or befriend at work. Do you make an effort to reach out to those who may not look like you or come from similar backgrounds? People from underrepresented groups often lack access to important networks. How can you help create more equitable access and ensure that each person with whom you work feels a sense of belonging? What advantages do you have that can be shared with others? Perhaps you have a skill to share, a connection to make, or a mentoring moment to share from something you've learned. Remember, it's a two-way street. You will likely learn and grow from the relationship in unique and surprising ways.

21. Is it fair to push back and be respectfully curious on some of the enlightened/woke perspectives, or does that just confirm a racial bias and white supremacy culture?

All perspectives and opinions should be valued and can be discussed, debated, and challenged. There is a spectrum of opinions when it comes to "wokeness," as everyone sees the world differently. Offer your opinion, as long as it's informed by a deep understanding of the issues at hand. When we jump to an angry, aggressive, or defensive posture, it's hard to listen or be heard. If we truly want to express our opinions and change hearts and minds, approaching these topics calmly, with thought and care, is typically the most effective way. If our goal is to build relationships, work to find essential points of concern and shared values and, perhaps for the moment, agree to disagree on the rest.

22. How do we encourage vulnerability in a "cancel culture" world?

To be canceled is to say or do something that the public deems distasteful or intolerable, often resulting in loss of support, opportunities, sales, and even a career. "Cancel culture" is divisive—on the one hand, it can limit free speech; on the other, it can hold people accountable for their words and actions. The consequences for missteps are real.

We've all seen people canceled for doing or saying things they didn't realize were wrong or offensive. And yet, if we don't step into courageous conversations, it's impossible to learn, grow, and understand the world from others' perspectives. These conversations require a certain amount of vulnerability—being willing to admit what you don't know, asking for help or clarification, and being willing to apologize when merited—even when your intent was not to offend.

Here are some tips for navigating today's cancel culture:

Be honest about what you know and don't know. Don't deny transgressions of the past. Vow to learn and grow from them. Authenticity and humility go a long way to building relationships and earning grace.

Be careful on social media and in other highly public venues. As you're stepping into new territory and courageous conversations, start your journey with one-on-one conversations.

Extend grace and compassion to others. None of us have a spotless past. Unless behavior is flagrantly offensive or abusive, assume the best of others, and seek to understand.

Humor can misfire, especially in written form. Joking about sensitive topics can often be misconstrued, so tread carefully. As grandma always said, don't put anything in writing that you wouldn't want read out loud in a deposition.

Weigh your options. Dr. Martin Luther King was canceled. 75% of Americans disapproved of him when he died. (SmithsonianMag.com)[7] What do you want to stand for? What impact do you seek? What are you willing to risk? Think about the elements of "time, place, manner, and relationship" when weighing your options.

---

[7] Cobb, James C. "Even Though He Is Revered Today, MLK Was Widely Disliked by the American Public When He Was Killed." Smithsonian Magazine, April 4, 2018. https://www.smithsonianmag.com/history/why-martin-luther-king-had-75-percent-disapproval-rating-year-he-died-180968664/.

SKEPTICISM

Check out our micro-podcasts on this topic

The Sources of Workplace Inequality: Prof. Donald Tomaskovic-Devey, UMass

Corporate Boards and the DEI Im

Being Inclusive at Work

Inclusivity is fundamentally about unleashing human potential. One of the most common reasons people leave jobs is because they feel underappreciated, unvalued, and unseen.

23. How do we create an environment for honest conversations, with opportunities for learning (and perhaps disagreement), and not an environment of judgment, shaming, and resentment?

To engage in honest conversations, it's critical to have psychological safety (see the chapter for Leaders and Managers). People must feel that their voice will be heard, respected, and valued (though not necessarily agreed with). To create this environment, it's best if the leader models and messages their own vulnerability. When we lead Inclusive Leadership sessions, we always ask the CEO to kick them off with an authentic story of a time when they messed up or felt like an "other."

Here are a few ways our clients have opened the sessions:

- A leader shared their story about showing up in a foreign country for a work meeting and being clueless about local customs—demonstrating a lack of cultural awareness and humility—and how that felt.
- One shared a conversation they had with an employee whose son had transitioned and the difficult life they faced, which helped this CEO develop empathy around pronoun use.
- A CEO, who grew up in an all-White community, shared their story of how they were racist until playing sports with Black teammates and connecting with their lived experience. This individual, who is committed to being an inclusive leader, demonstrates that anyone can evolve with awareness and intentionality.

These stories are powerful testaments to others in the organization about the value of humility, which is touted by Catalyst (a leading researcher) as the #1 trait of inclusive leaders.

Another way to create a safe and brave space for courageous conversations is to welcome feedback, whether positive or critical. By embracing a growth mindset and an interest in always learning, companies can send the signal that we are all works in progress, and none of us have it all figured out (and trust us, never will).

Encouraging risk-taking and not punishing failures is another way to create a culture of openness. Below is a summary of what fixed and growth mindsets look like in an organization. Those embracing a growth mindset are far more likely to have open, constructive conversations about tough topics. "You can measure the health of relationships, teams, and organizations by measuring the lag time between a problem emerging, and when it's honestly and effectively resolved," according to the book *Crucial Conversations*.[8]

---

[8] Patterson, Kerry, Joseph Grenny, Ron McMillan, and Al Switzler. *Crucial Conversations Tools for Talking When Stakes Are High, Second Edition*. McGraw Hill Professional, 2011.

MINDSETS IN ORGANIZATIONS

Fixed Mindset	Growth Mindset
"No, but"	"Yes, and"
Retribution for failure	Acknowledges failure
Slow to change	Always adapting
Risk-averse	Takes risks
Doesn't give feedback	Embraces feedback
Claims achievements	Shares achievements
Steals ideas/takes credit	Affirms others (microaffirmations)
Hides mistakes	Acknowledges mistakes
Ignores offers of help	Strong mentorship culture
"We've always done it this way"	" I wouldn't have thought of that!"
"They'll never change"	Believes people are coachable
Limited opportunities for growth	Invests in people development

24. I want to be an ally when I hear a racist, sexist, antisemitic or homophobic joke, but I don't really know what to say. What do you suggest?

Jokes that target an individual or group create harm and should not be tolerated in any space. Unfortunately, there will be instances when this type of behavior takes place. Be sure to respond in a manner that explicitly states that such behavior is disrespectful and not acceptable. Here are some options to consider:

- **"Call them in".** Reveal a bit more of yourself by speaking from your values. You can say something like, "I can't join you in finding humor in the comment you just made (or joke you just told), not only because I find it offensive to X person/group, but also because I know you're a more considerate (or some high-value quality that is true of them) person than that."

- **Call it out—now or later.** Speak up and tell the person that the joke is not appropriate. If you can do it immediately, that's often best. It allows the offender to know that you will not be a quiet bystander. It also reaffirms that it is hurtful and offensive to many people and has no place in your workplace or community. If it doesn't feel right to call it out in the moment, consider circling back with the individual later to have this conversation.

- **Explain why it's hurtful.** If possible, help the person understand why their joke is hurtful and offensive. Explain how it reinforces harmful stereotypes and contributes to discrimination and prejudice. If you are triggered, you might want to discuss this at another time and space.

- **If desired, support the impacted person(s).** If someone is hurt or offended by the joke, offer them support and let them know that you stand with them.
- **Set boundaries.** Let the person know that such behavior will not be tolerated in your workplace or community. Make it clear that discrimination and prejudice are not acceptable, and that there will be consequences for such behavior.

Jokes that demean, disrespect, and ridicule people should not be tolerated. Telling jokes and laughing can cause harm. By speaking up and addressing such behavior, you are helping to create a more inclusive and respectful environment for everyone.

Consider how Brené Brown approaches racist, sexist, or homophobic jokes, described in *Dare to Lead:* "Even if others are laughing, I'm not going to laugh. I'm going to ask you not to say that stuff around me. I don't do this out of self-righteousness or being 'better than'—trust me, there are times when I'd rather just shoot you a dirty look and walk away. I say something because courage is one of my key values, and for me to feel physically, emotionally, and spiritually okay, courage insists that I honor it by choosing my voice over my comfort."[9]

---

[9] Brown, Brené. *Dare to Lead: Brave Work. Tough Conversations. Whole Hearts.* Random House Publishing Group, 2018.

25. Everyone talks about the importance of "bringing your whole self to work." What if I don't *want* to bring my whole self to work?

While much of the discussion around building inclusive spaces of belonging revolves around this notion of bringing your whole self to work, not everyone feels similarly. For example, I (Alex) was told in a performance review that I needed to be more visible at evening events that revolved around drinking, in hopes that my team could get to know me better. As a single mother who didn't want to drink and felt the need to be home with my daughter in the evenings, this was not something I felt should be required in my role. However, recognizing the important of building relationships at work, I initiated lunches and coffee breaks during work hours to get to know my colleagues.

Others may choose to keep certain parts of their identities private, such as mental health struggles, home dynamics, and LGBTQ+ related topics.

26. What are the best methods to help overcome your own and others' unconscious biases?

It's important to note that we, as humans, are **all** biased. Biases can keep us safe and expedite decisions. But biases can also get in the way of making the best decisions or hiring the strongest talent.

To address our personal biases, it starts with awareness. Awareness doesn't happen without a healthy dose of self-reflection. We offer the following questions to ponder as a way of getting in touch with your own biases:

- ❏ How comfortable are you participating in diversity-related events or conversations?
- ❏ Do you correct racist, sexist, or homophobic comments or jokes?
- ❏ Do you stay current with blogs, articles, books, magazines, or news broadcasts from diverse authors and perspectives?
- ❏ Do you follow or interact with people on social media who hold different opinions and perspectives?
- ❏ Is your circle of friends diverse in their physical appearance, perspectives, and lifestyles?
- ❏ In the workplace, do you always eat lunch with people who look like you?
- ❏ In the workplace, do you mentor, network with, or sponsor people who look like you?

- Who are your "go-to" people in the workplace? Do they look and think like you?
- Are you a racism bystander or upstander? Are you an anti-racist?
- Where do your privileges/advantages exist? Where do you lack privilege/advantage? (e.g., socioeconomic status, education, skin color, ableism, sexual preference, gender)
- Do you intentionally educate yourself on diversity-related topics?
- Do you know the difference between prejudice, bias, and racism? Can you identify examples?
- Have you advocated for someone who was different from you? What was the outcome?

As further reflection, ask yourself these questions:

- If my first impression is negative, is my bias showing up?
- Do I listen to others share their experiences, even if I disagree with them?
- Do I lean in when others present conflicting views?
- Does my social or professional circle look and sound like me? If so, am I missing important perspectives?
- When someone is interrupted or spoken over, do I amplify their voice?
- When in a group or meeting, do I ensure all voices are heard?
- Am I more interested in sounding smart or in learning from others?
- Do I move more readily to curiosity or to judgment?

27. How do we treat people respectfully no matter their role, level, and whether I hired them or inherited them?

When you understand that being inclusive is really about being human and unleashing potential, it's much easier to really see people. Remembering names (and pronouncing them correctly); the names of spouses, partners, kids, and pets; and key events in their lives is one way to show you care. If you're not particularly good at this, consider taking notes in your contact manager or adding key dates to your calendar.

If you're a manager, conduct regular check-ins to ask how your employees are doing, both personally and professionally. Find out what they like about their job and what would make it better. Ask them what skills or superpowers they have that should be considered for future assignments. Ask what they see as their career path and how you can help. You may even ask what would make them leave the organization—a good question often included in a "stay interview." Introduce them to your networks and mentors who could help. These are all ways to treat people with respect and to inspire organizational loyalty.

28. How do I respectfully honor people's holidays when I don't fully understand what they're about?

We recently led a project for a client who wanted to attract and promote more Latin employees. In conducting focus groups, we heard that honoring their cultural traditions was a key part of making them feel included.

The first step is to educate yourself. A wealth of information exists on the internet. If you have a strong relationship with an employee whose traditions you are interested in learning about, respectfully ask them if they have the time to share their favorite customs. Then go the next step to honor these holidays by reaching out to employees who celebrate them. Recognize that a day off may be desired, or there may be food or other customs associated with that holiday that would be fun to share. Some companies host "Days of Understanding" to let employees share their cultural traditions and expand awareness for their colleagues.

29. What do I do when I innocently say something that offends someone?

It's important to acknowledge the difference between intent and impact. As mentioned earlier, when we have our foot out and accidentally trip someone, we didn't **intend** to trip them. Nevertheless, we apologize. The same goes for saying something to another person that doesn't land well. Even if you don't fully understand the offense, it's important to recognize the impact. Here are four steps we suggest you take:

- Acknowledge and apologize
- Take the time for personal reflection
- Offer to meet with the impacted individual(s)
- Be willing to be educated and learn from the experiences

Check out our micro-podcasts on this topic

Can Men Still Be Mentors To Women?	Do Women Need to be Better Salary Negotiators?
Can Cultural Holidays Be Celebrated at Work?	Is it okay for companies to capitalize on heritage month celebrations?
Are Today's Women Managers Burning Out?	Inclusive Leadership and Hispanic Heritage Month: Peter Muñiz of Home Depot
Do ERGs Help Employees… or Companies?	Putting People First and Hispanic Heritage Month: Leo Pacheco, Beacon

Being Inclusive Outside of Work

We included this chapter because while we believe we should consistently treat people with respect and dignity, whether at home or in the office, these questions are specific to scenarios one might face outside the workplace. In discussing these, please remember that a person's overall well-being is paramount. Be mindful of your triggers and avoid spaces that may cause distress. Use these guidelines in a way that works best for you.

30. Every year our family gets into a huge argument about something—whether it's global warming and climate change or the latest election. How can I have a respectful and fruitful conversation?

Start by thinking through your goals of the conversation. By being intentional about what you want to accomplish (and continuing to remind yourself of this when things get heated), it's easier to stay calm. To enter a difficult conversation without an intention is like walking in the forest without a compass.

When views are deeply entrenched, it's unreasonable to think you will change minds and hearts over a shared meal. Perhaps a better goal is to listen for any kernel of truth or agreement in their argument. It's also helpful to ask for facts to back up their beliefs. Saying "I'd like to understand your perspective. What's the basis for your belief?" can be a helpful way to listen. In the words of Bernard Baruch, "Everyone is entitled to his own opinion, but not to his own facts."

Remember that **listening** is the most important element of being a good conversationalist. If you continue to remind yourself that the goal is to listen, understand, and perhaps learn something (even if it's that your conversation partner doesn't have a leg to stand on), you will be more likely to keep calm. Also recognize when it's time to move on. If the conversation gets heated, perhaps it's best to agree to disagree and change the subject.

Here are some good listening tips, largely pulled from the ListenFirstProject.[10]

- Grant the courtesy of silence
- Use a calm and respectful tone
- Have an open mind, ready to learn and grow
- Remember the Platinum Rule—whenever possible, treat others how **they** want to be treated
- Be present and curious
- Fully engage
- Restate what you heard
- Ask respectful questions, free from judgment, assumption, or bias
- Discover common interests and areas of agreement

Most people would prefer to be with someone who's interest**ed** over interest**ing**. Consider asking probing questions and truly being present to hear their perspective. Always be aware of when you are **shifting** conversation to yourself versus **supporting** the other person. If they talk about their recent loss, don't shift the conversation to you and your recent loss. Support them by asking about the loss and simply listening. There's power in being heard.

Many of us engage in conversation about race, gender, politics, and religion not to grow our heart and understanding, but to confirm and persuade others on our own personal beliefs and convictions. Our goal is often to prove others wrong.

---

[10] "Listen First Project," April 6, 2023. https://www.listenfirstproject.org.

Consider changing your mindset when you enter a difficult conversation—approach it with curiosity and the intent to learn, or at the least to understand the basis of the other person's beliefs. You may be surprised at how much the conversation changes as a result.

Here are some good reminders when it comes to listening.

- Good listeners ask good questions
- Listening begets listening
- Listening does **not** mean you agree with someone (try saying "I hear you")
- One of the most gratifying things you can say to another person is: "I've been thinking about what you said."
- Vulnerability isn't weakness—it's power
- You can't be curious and on the attack at the same time
- Give your full attention (e.g., put your phone down, face the person speaking, make eye contact)
- Don't finish someone's sentences
- Don't rush to fill the silence—there's power in the pause
- Repeat specific feeling words: "I hear that. I understand your frustration."
- Practice supporting the speaker vs. shifting the conversation

31. My family is polarized on political issues. Do I even go there?

Political issues and other sensitive or emotion-driven topics can create hurt feelings, anger, alienation, high emotions, fractured relationships and disappointing outcomes. Consider your goal—are you trying to change hearts and minds, find points of agreement, or defend your point of view. Is this goal reasonable? Is it worth the risk? Here are some tips as you consider whether to "go there" with family and friends.

- **Time:** Is it the correct time? Can you pause the topic for another time?

- **Place:** Do you want to have a difficult conversation at the dining table? Should it be in a group or one-on-one? In-person or over the phone?

- **Manner:** Are you triggered? Would you be able to keep your composure? Would waiting and counting to 10 result in a more fruitful exchange?

- **Relationship:** What's your relationship with the individual(s)? Will you see them again? Do you interact on a regular basis? Are you comfortable severing a relationship with a family member over opposing views?

32. I want to be respectful of my newly out gay niece, but also don't want to make her uncomfortable. How do I talk about her choice in a way that builds connection? Or do I stay quiet until she brings it up?

Relationships are primary. Build a bridge to future conversation with your niece by acknowledging to her your awareness of her coming out. Affirm that you're open to conversation and sharing if she would like to at any time in the future. Allow your niece to discuss her sexuality with you in her own time. While your intentions are rooted in care for your niece, be respectful of her and what she wants to share with you. There are many helpful resources included at the end of this chapter for family and friends of people who identify as gay.

- Be respectful of their privacy
- Allow people the power to approach you and discuss their sexuality
- Educate yourself

33. My nephew goes by "they." I don't get it and don't agree with changing your gender. How do I handle this?

Your feelings are valid. In addition, your nephew's feelings are also valid. Consider the Platinum Rule: Whenever possible, treat others how **they** want to be treated. Using their preferred pronouns is one way of showing respect and care. As a family member, you can ask them questions for clarification. You can also educate yourself on pronoun usage to better understand why some people use various pronouns.

34. I'm bringing my Black girlfriend to my parents' (who are White) home for Thanksgiving. They will not receive this well. How do I prepare them, and how do I address issues that may arise over dinner?

In the words of Brené Brown, "being clear is kind, being unclear is unkind." Tell your family you will be bringing your girlfriend, a Black woman, to Thanksgiving. Allow them the opportunity to answer and acknowledge what you have said. If they are not comfortable, you can discuss how their discomfort impacts you. Let them know that you value both the family relationship and your relationship with your girlfriend, and you would like them to welcome and accept her. If it is clear they will not, you will need to make a difficult decision of bringing her anyway, going without her, or spending Thanksgiving with your girlfriend away from your family.

- Be intentional about expectations
- Allow people the chance to welcome change
- Be prepared to make difficult decisions if inclusion is not reached

35. My sister is just too "woke" for me. What should I do?

While the meaning of the term "woke" seems to change with each passing month, being "woke" generally means being alert to racial and social injustices. As humans, we should aspire to being more aware of equity and the various advantages many of us benefit from.

Most would agree that it's not pleasant to be stereotyped, especially as a stereotype that's been generated by meme culture. Seeing your sister as "too woke" doesn't reveal what is missing or what is challenging for you in your relationship with her. Ask yourself what "too woke" means for you and how that meaning, applied to your sister, gets in the way of being able to relate to each other from a place of care and consideration. Consider new ways to have a conversation with your sister to understand how each of your perspectives aligns or differs and to discover where you have shared values.

- Understand the definition of wokeness and how it positively shows up in society
- Unpack what is "too woke" for you. What is your trigger? What are you opposed to specifically?
- Have a conversation to discuss your viewpoints and better understand theirs

36. Is there a suggestion for a way to be inclusive of everyone at my dinner table? We have grandma who's 92 and grandchildren under 10.

There are many fun ways to include everyone around the table. One of our favorite traditions is to go around the table and have each person share a response to a question. Inevitably there's humor, tears, poignant moments, and touching memories. Kids as young as 3 or 4 can participate, and grandparents often have wisdom to share. It's a good idea to have the first person kick it off with something a bit vulnerable, which then amazingly sets the stage for others to follow suit. And a good rule for enhancing conversation and connection is to declare the dining table a technology-free zone.

There are plenty of other good conversation starters. Here are a few of our favorites:

- Describe one quality you admire about the person to your right.
- What's one thing you tried this year that was out of your comfort zone?
- What's one memory from the year that you will never forget?
- What's one goal you have for next year?
- What's one of the funniest moments you had this year?

37. I tend to hang out with people like me. It's comfortable and fun. Is this okay?

We all enjoy people who have common lived experiences, passions, hobbies, etc. But if our social circles are confined to those "like us," we are missing out on expanding our worldviews and our ability to enjoy and empathize with others. We come to a deeper recognition of our privileges when speaking with those whose experiences contrast our own. By listening to other perspectives (including authors, news channels, and publications), we benefit from expanded awareness, fresh thinking, cultural humility, and rich friendships.

BEING INCLUSIVE OUTSIDE OF WORK

Check out our micro-podcasts on this topic

Bringing Inclusive Practices from Work to the Thanksgiving Table

Gender Identity/Sexual Orientation

Navigating the ever-evolving guidelines around gender identity and sexual orientation can be challenging for many people. Here are some ways to create a more inclusive workplace.

38. How should I refer to a person from the LGBTQ+ community?

The proper way to refer to a person from the LGBTQ+ community is to use their name and pronoun, if they desire. The LGBTQ+ community is not monolithic, so use their name unless they mention a pronoun. If your goal is to create a more inclusive space, it is important to respect and acknowledge a person's gender identity and sexual orientation. It's not always appropriate to assume someone's gender identity, which is why pronouns can be useful.

It's also important to properly refer to people in virtual settings. It is now a common practice for people to include their pronouns with their names in those spaces. So when you enter a virtual room, be sure to check for people's names and pronouns.

39. Why do we need pronouns?

The use of pronouns is essential for communication. When we don't use someone's name, we need to substitute a pronoun. Many people who are in the process of gender transitioning or have already transitioned, as well as those who identify as androgynous, choose gender-neutral or gender-inclusive pronouns to self-identify.

Traditionally, singular pronouns are she/her/hers or he/him/his. In recent decades, the use of they/them/theirs as singular pronouns has become mainstream in referring to those whose gender isn't specified as well as for people who identify as non-binary. Although the singular "they" may seem ungrammatical to some, especially those who learned English a few decades ago, its use to refer to someone whose gender is unknown or irrelevant has been well established in English for centuries.

40. Should I ask for a person's pronoun when I meet them?

We are an ever-evolving society. It is becoming more common to see pronouns on name tags, email signatures, and virtual room screens. In 2020, Target gave all of its employees the option to put their pronouns on their nametags. You can now add your pronouns to your LinkedIn account so people will know how to address you.

When you meet people, especially in social settings, you cannot always assume their gender. Therefore, it is acceptable to ask for someone's pronouns. Be mindful that you want to be respectful and considerate when asking about pronouns. You may increasingly observe people opening meetings by using pronouns to create an inclusive space. For example, "Hi, I'm [name], and I use she/her pronouns. If you feel comfortable, please introduce yourself using your pronouns."

Using someone's pronouns is becoming more common and demonstrates that one's identity is valued. If you do make a mistake and use the wrong pronoun, apologize and make a genuine effort to use the correct pronoun going forward.

41. What if I'm not comfortable using pronouns and want to call someone how I see them?

In order to properly answer this question, it's important that we understand the Platinum Rule. We often hear about the Golden Rule—Treat others how **you** want to be treated. The Platinum Rule is to, whenever possible, treat others how **they** want to be treated. Using correct pronouns is an essential aspect of respecting someone's identity. If you choose not to use someone's preferred pronouns, you risk misgendering them, which can be hurtful and invalidating. Someone's physical appearance can appear to be in contrast with their chosen pronouns. If you strive to be an inclusive leader, it is important to respect people's choices in this regard.

42. What does LGBTQ+ or LGTBQIA mean?

LGBTQ+ stands for Lesbian, Gay, Bisexual, Transgender, and Queer. The + sign represents other sexual identities such as Questioning, Intersex, or Asexual. Queer is an umbrella term that is now widely used to refer to the LGBTQ+ community.

43. What can I do to help members of my team, family, or friends who may be transitioning or coming out?

It's important to understand that help or assistance could be different for everyone. There might be a team member who does not want support and would rather stick to professional boundaries. However, there might be a team member that will welcome your support as they transition or come out. The following suggestions are not finite and should be heavily weighed in accordance with workplace policies and procedures. Here are some things you can do to help:

- **Educate yourself.** Take the time to educate yourself about the experiences of LGBTQ+ people, including the challenges they may face when coming out or transitioning. This can help you better understand and empathize with your team members and help you provide appropriate support.

- **Create a brave and welcoming environment.** Make sure that your workplace is inclusive and welcoming to all employees, regardless of their sexual orientation or gender identity. This can include promoting diversity and inclusion policies, providing gender-neutral bathrooms, and encouraging (but not mandating) the use of preferred pronouns (e.g., email signatures, name tags).

- **Be an active listener.** If someone on your team is struggling with coming out or transitioning, be a good listener and offer your support. Encourage them to share their experiences, and let them know that you are there to help.

- **Respect their privacy.** It is important to respect people's privacy and autonomy when it comes to their gender identity and sexual orientation. Only share information that they have explicitly given you permission to share.
- **Provide resources.** Provide your team members with resources and support networks that can help them navigate their coming out or transition process. This may include LGBTQ+ organizations, counseling services, and support groups. Also check with your company's human resources department for internal company resources.

Remember, the most important thing you can do to support others is to be a compassionate and supportive ally.

It can be scary, challenging, and emotionally activating to discuss one's LGBTQ+ identity with friends or family. Be supportive and understanding and try not to create a "fixing" solution. This can be a process and might take multiple courageous conversations.

Remember, being LGBTQ+ inclusive is an ongoing process of learning, growth, and advocacy. According to the Harvard Business Review, *being an ally is a strategic mechanism used by individuals to become collaborators, accomplices, and co-conspirators who fight injustice and promote equity in the workplace through supportive personal relationships and public acts of sponsorship and advocacy.* This definition can be your reminder to be strategic and continuous in your journey to be more inclusive to the LGBTQ+ community.

RESOURCES TO SUPPORT THE LGBTQ+ COMMUNITY

- **PFLAG** (Parents, Families and Friends of Lesbians and Gays): PFLAG is a national organization that provides support, education, and advocacy for LGBTQ+ individuals and their families. They offer support groups, educational resources, and community events.

- **The Trevor Project:** The Trevor Project is a national organization that provides crisis intervention and suicide prevention services to LGBTQ+ youth. They also offer resources for parents and families to help support LGBTQ+ youth.

- **The Matthew Shepard Foundation:** This foundation created The Laramie Project, which is a national play to bring awareness to the killing of Matthew Shepard, a gay man killed in Laramie, Wyoming, because of his sexual orientation.

- **GLAAD:** GLAAD is an LGBTQ+ media advocacy organization that provides resources and information on how to support LGBTQ+ individuals and families.

- **Human Rights Campaign:** The Human Rights Campaign is a national organization that advocates for LGBTQ+ rights and provides resources and support for families.

- **Gender Spectrum:** Gender Spectrum is an organization that provides education, training, and support for families, schools, and professionals working with gender-expansive and transgender youth.

- **Local LGBTQ+ community centers:** Many local LGBTQ+ community centers offer support groups and resources for families of LGBTQ+ individuals.
- **Local universities and/or community colleges:** Many institutions offer free programming, events, and resources for members of the LGBTQ+ community. Check out Campus Pride for a comprehensive list.

Global Awareness

Understanding the impact on globalization in the workplace is essential to building an inclusive workplace and being a more conscious leader.

44. What is cultural intelligence?

Are you familiar with other cultures besides your own? Understanding cultural intelligence (CQ) is the first step in being a global inclusive citizen. Having cultural intelligence is the ability to understand, appreciate, and effectively work with people from diverse cultural backgrounds. In order to develop cultural intelligence, it's important to be cognizant of and responsive to cultural differences, and have the skills to adapt to new and unfamiliar cultural contexts. For example, when you travel to other countries, do you learn about their customs and traditions?

Cultural intelligence includes <u>several key components</u>,[11] such as:

- **Cultural knowledge:** This refers to understanding the beliefs, values, and practices of different cultures. For example, being familiar with symbols, colors, geography, religious customs, and holidays associated with a culture.

- **Cultural mindfulness:** This involves being aware of one's own cultural biases and assumptions, and recognizing the potential impact these may have on interactions with people from other cultures. Consider how you feel about people from different cultures and your own stereotypes, biases, and beliefs.

- **Cultural skills:** These are the abilities to communicate, negotiate, and build relationships with people from

---

[11] Delaney. "Developing Cultural Intelligence at Work & Why It Matters." *Red Thread Brands*, May 24, 2022. <u>https://www.redthreadbrands.com/blog/developing-cultural-intelligence-at-work-why-it-matters/</u>.

different cultural backgrounds. Learning a different language is one way to expand your cultural skills.

- **Cultural motivation:** This involves a genuine interest in learning about and engaging with other cultures, as well as a willingness to adapt one's own behaviors and attitudes to better align with cultural norms.

Having cultural intelligence is also a smart business practice. According to the Bureau of Economic Analysis, in 2019 U.S. multinational corporations earned over $4.2 trillion in revenue from their foreign operations. Developing cultural intelligence is essential in today's globalized world, as it enables individuals and organizations to effectively navigate cross-cultural interactions and achieve success in multicultural environments.

45. What do you mean by cultural "humility"?

As consultants, we learn, teach, and educate about the practice of being an inclusive leader. Although we are steeped in this work, we try to embody humility, recognizing there is no "diversity and inclusion finish line." This thinking is core to the notion of cultural humility and the recognition that we will always be lifelong learners in regard to other cultures.

Cultural humility emphasizes the importance of approaching intercultural interactions with an attitude of openness, curiosity, and vulnerability. It involves recognizing the limits of one's own knowledge and experiences, and acknowledging that other people's cultural perspectives and experiences may differ from our own. Your lived experience is not always the only true and right one.

Unlike cultural competence or cultural intelligence, which may suggest mastery or expertise in other cultures, cultural humility acknowledges that we can never truly be experts in someone else's culture or fully understand their experiences. Cultural humility is awareness and presence that allows one to enter into cultural interactions with a degree of respect and appreciation and with the mindset to learn.

Here are some tips to help increase your cultural humility:

- **Self-reflection:** We all have biases. Are you aware of your biases and how they impact how you interact with others? Having self-reflection involves understanding one's own cultural background and biases, and then recognizing that a lack of information about others can impact decisions.

- **Respectful communication:** This involves being an active listener and being respectful of others. If you ask questions, be respectfully curious.

- **Open-mindedness:** This involves being open to different perspectives and ways of thinking, and recognizing that there is always more to learn about other cultures and experiences.

- **Embrace being a lifelong learner:** This involves an ongoing commitment to learning about other cultures and experiences, and a willingness to continually challenge and question one's own assumptions and biases.

Being an inclusive leader is important in both business and personal relationships. Practicing cultural humility is a soft skill that you can grow, and it can assist you in being a stronger leader, colleague, and friend.

46. It's easier for me to collaborate with people who speak English as their first language. I often pick them to be on my project. Is this a form of bias?

We all have biases, and this is a form of bias. Let's identify it and then discuss how to mitigate its unintended outcomes going forward.

First, if you consistently select people who speak English as their first language to collaborate with, you are potentially excluding people who do not speak English as their first language, even if they may be just as qualified or even more qualified for the project. This type of bias is known as linguistic bias or language-based bias, and it is a form of cultural bias.

It is important to recognize that language proficiency is not always a reflection of someone's competence, expertise, or potential contributions to a project. You often hear the term ESL, which means English as a Second Language; however, consider ESOL, which is English to Speakers of Other Languages. ESOL implies that many people might not be proficient in English but are able to speak two or three languages—they are multilingual. Therefore, having a bias against someone based on language could hinder your learning about other languages and cultures.

To reduce linguistic bias and promote diversity and inclusion in your collaborations, it is important to intentionally seek out and include individuals from diverse language and cultural backgrounds, and to provide support and accommodations for individuals who may have different language needs. Additionally, you can work to improve your own cultural intelligence and language skills to better communicate and collaborate with people from diverse backgrounds.

47. **I work on a global team and many of my colleagues have different political views based on their culture. Each time they get into debates, I know it has the potential to erupt and damage relationships. Should I be shutting these conversations down?**

Robust debate and courageous conversations can be healthy for a workplace. However, it is imperative that you have the resources and tools to help people have those conversations. Disrespect, demeaning words, and ridicule could cause more harm than good when having courageous conversations. It may be appropriate to set aside a specific time to discuss sensitive topics such as religion, politics, or social justice issues in the workplace. In our work, we interact with companies who hold "Belonging Chats," where employees are introduced to a brave space to discuss sensitive topics and ask vulnerable questions.

If you decide to hold these debates, it may be appropriate for you to have ground rules such as:

- Confidentiality: no recordings or video
- Respect: every voice is valued
- Judgment-free zone
- Compassion
- All questions are valid
- Vulnerability is a strength
- Be an active listener
- Practice cultural humility

Ultimately, the goal is to promote a collaborative and respectful work environment where people feel comfortable sharing their opinions and perspectives, but also know when to respect each other's differences and focus on their shared goals and objectives.

48. **If you have a foreign coworker, how do you balance being curious about their home country and culture while not wanting to ask a question that may be considered a microaggression (such as "where are you from?")**

    Globalization has an impact on workplace cultures. In today's society, you are more than likely working with people from other countries. It is imperative to practice cultural humility and have a growth mindset. We encourage stepping into courageous conversations, being an active listener, and asking respectfully curious questions. Here are some examples of questions that you might want to ask:

    - "I was reading about (insert topic) and I wanted to ask you about some of the cultural traditions or customs that are important in your home country? Are you open to sharing this with me?"
    - "It has been a pleasure working with you. What inspired you to pursue your career path, and how does your cultural background influence your approach to work?"
    - "I recognize that we are in different time zones. What are some of the challenges you've faced working in a United States-based company?"

    It is important to avoid making assumptions about your coworker based on their appearance or accent, or asking questions that may be considered insensitive or intrusive, such as "Where are you really from?" or "I heard that everyone in your country believes xxx." Instead, focus on asking questions that express a genuine interest in their experiences and perspectives, and that respect their boundaries and cultural differences. Starting with "what" or "how" is often a better approach than "why," as "why" can put people on the defensive and suggest judgment on behalf of the questioner.

Finally, it is important to be an active listener, to ask respectful questions, and to avoid stereotypes. You can foster psychological safety and respectful dialogue when you practice these strategies.

49. Should I bow when I meet my Asian colleagues?

There are over 50 Asian countries, and they are not monolithic. Bowing is a common gesture of respect in many Asian cultures, but it is not necessarily expected or appropriate in all situations. Whether or not to bow when meeting your Asian colleagues will depend on the specific cultural norms and expectations of the individual or group you are interacting with, as well as the context and setting of the meeting.

If you are uncertain about whether to bow when meeting your Asian colleagues, it may be helpful to observe how they greet each other and then follow their lead. Alternatively, you could consider asking your colleagues directly about their cultural customs and expectations, while expressing a genuine interest in learning more about their culture and background. Also, consider using technology. YouTube and TikTok have many videos and tutorials on how to interact in Asian countries.

50. How can I be more inclusive of faith traditions, such as those of my Muslim colleagues who honor Ramadan?

Ramadan is a Muslim holy month of worship, study, prayer, fasting, reflection, and community gathering. It is the ninth month of the Islamic calendar, so the exact dates of observance vary year to year. As an inclusive leader, it is important to know the dates of Ramadan for the current year.

During Ramadan, Muslims fast from sunrise to sunset and may experience physical and mental fatigue, which could impact their ability to perform certain tasks. We all want to be helpful, but making assumptions about the needs of your Muslim colleagues is not beneficial in the workplace. There are ways to be sensitive to other cultures while simultaneously not directly targeting a specific demographic. For example, make sure that Ramadan is on the company-wide calendar as a cultural holiday.

If you have a close relationship with Muslim colleagues, ask them what their needs are during Ramadan. By approaching the topic in this way, you are acknowledging your Muslim colleagues' cultural and religious practices—company-wide and personal—while also showing a willingness to be flexible and accommodating to their needs. It is important to listen actively and respectfully to their responses, and to work collaboratively to find solutions that work for everyone. In addition, be aware of other religious practices such as prayer, cultural attire, and religious calendar observances.

Some some considerations when working with global teams:

- If time zones make for inconvenient meeting times, consider trading off meeting times so one territory doesn't always have to meet early in morning or late at night.

- Given the inconvenience of some meeting times for certain geographies, consider which meetings must be face to face and which issues could be handled in other ways, perhaps asynchronously.

- Write down agenda items, questions, and deadlines to avoid language confusion (written communication is generally easier to understand than spoken).

- Ask for clarification to ensure that language barriers aren't getting in the way. Consider slowing down your speaking.

- Consider whether language proficiency is a critical skill when hiring.

- Consider cultural traditions which may include hierarchies, castes, and gender roles and may inhibit some from speaking up in meetings.

- Recognize each other's holidays as a way to build relationships; be mindful of proposing meetings on cultural and religious holidays.

- If some voices are more timid, find other ways to ensure they are heard—such as asking them individually before or after meetings; be mindful of calling them out in a meeting as this is not always comfortable in some cultures.

- In some cultures, people are taught not to speak if they are not the senior person in the room. Others may feel embarrassed or uncomfortable speaking because they don't feel their language skills are proficient. Sometimes waiting uncomfortably long after asking a question is a smart strategy.

- Be liberal with micro affirmations and show appreciation, but ask or observe how they like to be recognized. Individuals in some cultures do not enjoy the limelight and prefer private acknowledgement of good work.

- Recognize and credit the originator of ideas.

- Pay attention to names and use them correctly—write down the pronunciation phonetically if it's a name you're not familiar with so you get it right going forward and don't need to ask them to repeat it.

- Respect personal boundaries—some cultures are more open than others when it comes to personal sharing.

Inclusive Language Guide

These guidelines help create inclusive cultures and safe spaces.

INSTEAD OF SAYING...	CONSIDER...
GENDERED LANGUAGE	**GENDER-NEUTRAL LANGUAGE** (when possible)
Businessman, Chairman	Businessperson, Chair
Salesman	Salesperson
Maternity/Paternity leave	Family leave, Parental leave
Man hour, Man month	Person hour, Person month
Manpower	Labor, workforce, personnel, employees
Boyfriend, girlfriend	Partner
Husband, wife	Spouse, partner
Manmade	Synthetic, artificial, manufactured
Workmanship	Craft, skill
Transgendered	Transgender
"They'll never change"	Believes people are coachable
Limited opportunities for growth	Invests in people development

BIASED LANGUAGE Avoid referring to race/ethnicity unnecessarily and never use a racial slur. Avoid using color as a positive or negative attribute.	BIAS-FREE LANGUAGE
Black market, Blacklist, Whitelist	Illegal market, Blocklist, Allowlist
Flesh-colored, Skin-colored, nude	Use precise color
Grandfather clause	Legacy
Master/Slave	Primary/Subordinate
Minority/Marginalized	Underrepresented group
DISABILITY-FOCUSED	**PERSON-FOCUSED AND DISABILITY AWARE**
Disabled person	Person with disability
Handicapped person	Person with disability
Able-bodied, healthy, normal, regular	Person without disabilities
Deaf person	Is deaf or hearing impaired
Blind person	Is blind or visually impaired
Dumb/mute	Is unable to speak
Suffers from/is victim of	Has (condition)
Retarded/slow	Has cognitive disabilities
Sanity check	Final check/quality check
AGE BIASED Don't describe older people as frail, weak, or in need of protection. Likewise, don't describe all young people as inexperienced, needy, or overindulged. Be careful about stereotyping.	**AGE RESPECTED**
Elderly	Older adult/person
Youthful/young	Vibrant/energized

Inclusive Practices

Know yourself

- It starts with your mindset. Are you committed to being inclusive?
- Be aware of your biases
- When you observe biases, ask yourself: What is this belief based on?
- Continue to read articles/blogs, listen to podcasts, and educate yourself

Get to know others

- Pronounce names correctly (ask if unsure)
- Use their chosen pronouns
- Recognize and respect the needs of neurodiverse individuals (ADHD, speech impediments, autism)
- Find out about their hobbies/passions
- Remember key events (weddings, babies, graduations, surgery, etc.)
- Check in on any events that may impact them or their families (hurricanes, crimes, wars, social justice issues)
- Take time to be present and listen

Run inclusive meetings

- Has everyone had a chance to speak?
- Consider speaking last and calling on others to share their perspectives first
- Seek out feedback from those who aren't comfortable speaking up or who are remote
- Recognize that language and cultural barriers may hold people back
- Ask yourself: "What perspectives are missing?"
- Recognize that internal processors may need more time and space to share their thoughts
- Get to know others

Other steps to take

- Be curious, not judgmental
- Practice "micro affirmations"
- Mentor someone who doesn't look like you
- Expand your personal and professional networks to develop greater empathy and understanding
- Step into allyship when you hear inappropriate comments or jokes or when someone is being interrupted

Acknowledgements

We are deeply grateful to the many individuals who have contributed their wisdom and support to bring this book to fruition.

Special thanks to Tara DeNuccio, Patty White, and Kara Powell, whose editorial insights and generosity of time have helped create a work that we hope will benefit many. We are also indebted to Wes Cowley, who edited our first book and consistently offers sharp, invaluable feedback on our writing. To Chris Riback, our colleague and dear friend, who has always challenged us to raise our game and improve our craft. We extend our heartfelt thanks to David Fasold for his encouragement and willingness to lend his expertise to our work whenever possible.

To our clients, we are grateful for the opportunity to learn and grow alongside you on this journey.

Last but not least, we would like to thank our families, who have supported us through every step of this endeavor. Your unwavering encouragement and patience have been invaluable as we work to create a world we can all be proud to live in.

For Diane's family—Mark, Lisa, Christine, and Matt—thank you for putting up with me and my many questions, favors, and requests. You are my reason for being.

From Alex to Emory, my walking heartbeat. Thank you for being "my favorite child" and always keeping me humble and current.

KEEP THE CONVERSATION GOING

WE WOULD LOVE TO HEAR FROM YOU

Please use the following ways to connect:

Diane.Flynn@ReBootAccel.com

Alex.White@ReBootAccel.com

Anonymous Text Line: 662-715-3588

ReBootAccel.com

Callinpodcast.com

Additional resources:

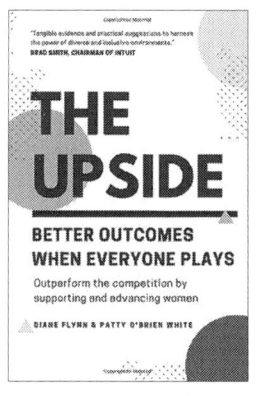

About the Authors

Diane Flynn is cofounder and CEO of ReBoot Accel, designing inclusive work cultures. She consults with Fortune 500 companies, coaches executives, and facilitates workshops that support and promote women and underrepresented groups. She co-authored *The Upside*, presenting the business case for diverse workforces and best practices for tapping the potential of women. She facilitates workshops for alumni at Stanford Business School and serves as guest faculty at the Modern Elder Academy and 1440 Multiversity. She has been featured on The Today Show, NBC's Morning Joe, ABC News, NPR's The Takeaway, WSJ, and Forbes, and also has the top-selling course at Udemy on the Growth Mindset. Diane was previously Chief Marketing Officer of GSVlabs, VP Business Development at Electronic Arts, and an associate consultant at the Boston Consulting Group. She earned a BA in economics from Stanford and an MBA from Harvard.

Diane is the mother of three, and lives with her husband in Menlo Park, California.

Dr. Alexandria White is Senior Vice President for Diversity, Equity and Inclusion at ReBoot Accel. She has been delivering training around diversity, leadership, and social justice since

2005. Alex consults with organizations on ways to create a more diverse and inclusive workplace. She founded S.A.M.S. (Student Affairs MomS), the largest online community for mothers who work in the student affairs profession. Her professional career has involved retail banking, servant leadership, community activism, diversity planning, and higher education. Alex is adjunct faculty in the School of Education at the University of Mississippi, and is a frequent speaker and podcast guest. She co-hosts a podcast called Call In, providing advice to business leaders on being an inclusive leader. She holds a BA from Indiana University, an MA from Ball State University and a EdD from University of Mississippi.

Alex has one daughter and enjoys extreme activities such as skydiving, parasailing, and ziplining. She is originally from Chicago, Illinois, but currently resides in Oxford, Mississippi.

Made in the USA
Monee, IL
05 September 2023